BIBLE 309
GOD WANTS MAN T[...]

CONTENTS

Author: Patricia Goss, M.A.
Editor-in-Chief: Richard W. Wheeler, M.A.Ed.
Editor: Joyce Andrews Davis
Consulting Editor: John L. Booth, Th.D.
Revision Editor: Alan Christopherson, M.S.

Alpha Omega Publications®

804 N. 2nd Ave. E., Rock Rapids, IA 51246-1759

Learn with our friends:

 When you see me, I will help your teacher explain the exciting things you are expected to do.

 When you do actions with me, you will learn how to write, draw, match words, read, and much more.

 You and I will learn about matching words, listening, drawing, and other fun things in your lessons.

GOD WANTS MAN TO HELP MAN

Everyone in the world has important work to do. In this LIFEPAC® you will learn what that important work is. You will also learn why it is important for you to do your work.

Objectives

Read these objectives. They will tell you what you will be able to do when you have finished this LIFEPAC.

1. You will be able to tell who you are to care for.
2. You will be able to tell who your brothers and sisters are.
3. You will be able to name six ways you are to treat others.
4. You will be able to tell two reasons why you should serve others.
5. You will be able to tell three ways the Lord will take care of you.

6. You will be able to recite Ephesians 4:32, First John 4:11, and Philippians 4:6 and 7.

Biblia (bēb′ lē u). The word Bible in Spanish.

eternal (i tėr′ nul). Lasting forever.

Jesucristo (hā′ sü krēs′ tō). The word Jesus Christ in Spanish.

Mexico (meks′ u kō). A country south of the United States.

serve (sėrv). To work for others.

supplication (sup′ lu kā′ shun). To ask for something.

These words will appear in **boldface** (darker print) the first time they are used.

Pronunciation Key: hat, āge, cãre, fär; let, ēqual, tėrm; it, īce; hot, ōpen, ȯrder; oil; out; cup, pu̇t, rūle; child; long; thin; /ᴛʜ/ for then; /zh/ for measure; /u/ represents /a/ in about, /e/ in taken, /i/ in pencil /o/ in lemon, and /u/ in circus.

I. WHO AM I TO CARE FOR?

It is very easy to care for people you know and love. Is it easy to care for people you do not know or you do not like? God tells you in His Word who you are to care for.

Biblia	(bēb' lē u)	The word Bible in Spanish.
Jesucristo	(hā' sü krēs' tō)	The word Jesus Christ in Spanish.
Mexico	(meks' u kō)	A country south of the United States.
serve	(sėrv)	To work for others

Ask your teacher to say these words with you.
Teacher check _____

Initial   Date

ALL PEOPLE ARE GOD'S CREATION

Walking down the street, eight-year-old Rosa felt very lonely. She had just moved into a new house and had not made any friends yet. Rosa was sad when she remembered her friends at her other house.

Rosa's family had just moved to the United States from **Mexico**. Her mama had told her that soon she would have new friends and feel happy again. Rosa was not very sure it would be true. She did not speak very much English, so it would be hard for her to talk with the boys and girls in her new school and neighborhood.

Rosa's papa spoke English well and wanted to teach Rosa. But papa was very busy with his new job.

Rosa did have one special friend to whom she could always talk. He understood every language. His name is **Jesucristo**. Rosa had trusted in Jesus as her savior when she was seven years old. Now she thought about how happy she was to be a Christian. She was really never alone.

Draw a circle around all the right answers.

1.1   Who was Rosa's friend?

Papa   Jesucristo   girls

1.2   Being a Christian made Rosa's_____ happy.

school   neighborhood   life

1.3   Rosa was never really _____.

sad   happy   alone

1.4   Jesucristo understood _____.
        every language   some things   a few things
1.5   Jesucristo means _____ in Spanish.
        Jesse Crist   Jesus Christ   a friend

That night Rosa asked her mama how she could make friends. She was going to the new school for the first time in the morning.

Mama told Rosa not to be afraid. She told her to smile and be friendly to everyone. She told her to listen carefully and try to learn the new language. Mama reminded Rosa to ask Jesucristo to help her. Mama opened the big family **Biblia** and read (Ephesians 4:32), "And be ye kind one to another, tenderhearted [feeling kind], forgiving one another, even as God for Christ's sake hath forgiven you."

The next morning Rosa left for school, waving goodbye to Mama. At school the teacher smiled and told the boys and girls to help Rosa learn to speak English better.

That afternoon Rosa went home very sad. The boys and girls had not been kind to her. They had not helped her. Rosa was upset with the boys and girls who made fun of her.

Mama heard Rosa crying and asked her what made her so unhappy. Rosa told her Mama about her bad day at school. She told her she did not want to go back again.

Mama asked Rosa to look up Ephesians 4:32 again in the Biblia.

Find Ephesians 4:32 and answer these questions.

1.6   How does God say to treat one another?

_____

1.7   How does God say we should feel about one another?_____

1.8   What does God say to do to others who are not kind to you?_____

1.9   Why does God say to forgive others?_____

        _____

1.10   Why has God forgiven you?_____

        _____

_____

Papa heard Mama talking and wanted to help Rosa. He said that God had created everyone. Papa told Rosa six ways that God wanted her to treat others.

1. **Serve** others.
2. Show God's love to others.
3. Tell others about Jesus.
4. Share with others.
5. Forgive others.
6. Be kind to others even when they are not kind to you.

Papa told Rosa to go back to school thinking about the ways God wanted her to treat others. Rosa wanted to please her papa, her mama, and God. She said that she would try.

Draw a line to what God wanted Rosa to do.

What happened at school	What God wants Rosa to do
1.11 Judy left her lunch at home. Rosa could eat all her own lunch or	serve.
1.12 Tom said he was sorry for being mean. Rosa could be angry or	tell others about Jesus.
1.13 Sally spilled her milk. Rosa could not help her clean it or	show God's love.
1.14 Mary made a face at Rosa. Rosa could make a face back or	forgive.
1.15 John asked Rosa why she was nice to people who were mean to her. Rosa could say, "I don't know" or	share.
1.16 Rosa's teacher said that Rosa must stay after school to learn more English. Rosa could act angry about staying or	be kind to the unkind.

Draw a circle around the correct word.

1.17   I want to (wear, where) the white shirt today.

1.18   I am going to give my mother the pink (flower, flour) to put in her hair.

1.19   Have you (red, read) this book about horses yet?

1.20   The wind (blew, blue) the papers all around.

1.21   We like to (sew, so) clothes for my big sister.

1.22   Some people are (to, too, two) tall to fit in this car.

1.23   Did you (no, know) that I like to go boating?

1.24   He hurt his (toe, tow) on that rock.

1.25   One black (bare, bear) in the zoo is very lazy.

Fill in the missing vowels to name six ways you should treat others.

1.26   S__rv__.

1.27   Sh__r__.

1.28   T__ll __th__rs __b____t J__s__s.

1.29   F__rg__v__.

1.30   B__ k__nd t__ th__ __nk__nd.

1.31   Sh__w G__d's l__v__.

Write a sentence telling how you will do each of these six things this week.

1.32 _____

1.33 _____

1.34 _____

1.35 _____

1.36 _____

1.37 _____

Rosa came home from school feeling much better. She was thinking it was funny that she felt better the next day because she still did not have any friends. Mama and Papa saw her coming and went out to meet her. They asked her if she had a good day. She told them how she treated the boys and girls. She told them how Jesucristo helped her to be kind to the unkind. Mama and Papa were very happy for Rosa. They knew God was with their little girl.

Write why you think Rosa felt better.

1.38 _____

Teacher check _____
                       Initial   Date

God wants all of His children to forgive others. Are you a Christian? Is there someone that you need to forgive? You may write him a letter forgiving him or ask him to forgive you if you have been unkind. You will feel better and God will be happy with you. Is there someone you need to thank? Write him a letter thanking him now.

ALL CHRISTIANS ARE BROTHERS AND SISTERS

Now Rosa was learning to speak the English language. She still played by herself much of the time. Some of the boys and girls were friendly. She had to remember to be kind to those who were not kind to her. She often asked Jesucristo to help her.

Rosa wanted a Christian friend. She wanted a friend who was part of God's family. Rosa knew that everyone who trusted in Jesus as their Savior was her brother or sister in the Lord. Rosa told her mama she wanted a Christian friend who would love God through Jesucristo. She wanted a friend that belonged to the family of God.

Draw a circle around all the sentences that show Rosa is a Christian.

1.39   Rosa was born into a family that goes to church.

1.40   Rosa trusted in Jesucristo as her Savior.

1.41   Rosa is a good girl.

1.42   Rosa prays to God through Jesucristo.

1.43   Rosa thanks God through Jesucristo.

1.44   Rosa's papa is a Christian.

1.45   Rosa loves God through Jesucristo.

1.46   Rosa belongs to the family of God through Jesucristo.

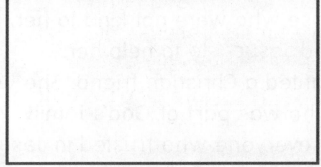

Recite Ephesians 4:32 to a friend.

1.47   Draw a red heart in the box if you can say the verse from memory perfectly.

Teacher check _____

                    Initial   Date

Review REVIEW Review

For this Self Test, study what you have read and done. The Self Test will check what you remember.

SELF TEST 1

Write the missing words and number.

1.01   "And a. _____ ye b. _____ one to
        another, c. _____ , d _____ one
        e. _____ , even as f. _____ for
        g. _____ sake hath forgiven h. _____."
        Ephesians 4: i. _____

Draw a circle around every correct answer. Some have
more than one correct answer.

1.02   I am to care for _____ .
        good people   everyone   Christians

1.03   My brothers and sisters in God's family are
        _____ .
        everyone   good people   Christians

1.04   I can love others because of _____ .
        Jesucristo   Jesus   Mother

1.05   All _____ are God's creation.
        Christians   good   people

1.06   God wants me to _____ others.
        love   serve   forgive

13 (thirteen)

1.07   Only brothers and sisters in God's family can
                _____ together through Jesus.

                work   pray   play

1.08   Brothers and sisters are in God's family through

                _____ .

                helping   forgiving   Jesus Christ

Complete the six ways God wants you to treat others.

1.09   S_____ .

1.010   Sh_____ .

1.011   F_____ .

1.012   B____ k____ t____ the u_____ .

1.013   T____ o_____ a____ J_____ .

1.014   S____ G____ l____ t____ o_____ .

Write four things Christians may do together through Jesus Christ.

1.015   L_____ G_____ .

1.016   P_____ to G_____ .

1.017   T_____ G_____ .

1.018   B_____ to the f_____ of G_____ .

33 / 41

EACH ANSWER, 1 POINT

Teacher Check _____
                          Initial   Date

My Score

14 (fourteen)

II. WHY SHOULD I SERVE OTHERS?

Do you always want your own way? Many people do. Study this part of the LIFEPAC to see how God wants you to live.

eternal	(i tėr' nul)	Lasting forever.

GOD LOVES ME

Rosa sat next to a girl at school named Sally. The girls had become friends. One day when Rosa had needed help with some schoolwork, the teacher had asked Sally to help Rosa. Sally did not want to give up her free time to help Rosa. As Sally worked with Rosa, she found out what a kind girl Rosa was. Sally also saw how Rosa forgave her for not wanting to help her. Soon Rosa and Sally began playing together and eating lunch together.

Sally worked with Rosa.

One day Sally went home with Rosa after school to play. Sally liked Rosa's mama and papa. Sally told Rosa that something was special about her family. Sally asked Rosa what made them different.

Rosa saw the big Biblia on the table. The Bible made her think about Jesucristo who was always with her and Mama and Papa.

She reached for the Biblia and read Ephesians 4:32 to Sally.

Mama came in and told Sally to look up First John 4:11. Rosa read it to Sally, too. "Beloved, if God so loved us, we ought [a duty] also to love one another."

Learn this Bible verse.

2.1 Write First John 4:11 on the lines exactly as it is written in the Bible. Learn it and say it to a friend.

_____

_____

Teacher check _____

name

Answer these questions.

2.2 Where did Rosa meet Sally?_____

2.3 What did the teacher ask Sally to do with Rosa?

_____

2.4 How did Sally feel about having to help Rosa?

_____

_____

2.5 Who saw what a kind girl Rosa was?_____

2.6 What did Rosa do to show she was kind?_____

_____

Now Sally knew why Rosa did not fight back and say unkind words to others. Sally asked how she could become a Christian. Rosa told Sally that she should tell God that she believed Jesucristo was the Son of God and died to give her **eternal** life.

Sally prayed these words to God. Then she smiled at Rosa and her mama. They smiled back at her. Sally was now part of the family of God. Sally and Rosa made pretty posters to hang in their rooms.

Make a poster for your room.

2.7 Color in the background. Then cover the letters with glue and glitter. Cut out the poster and glue it onto some heavy, colored paper.

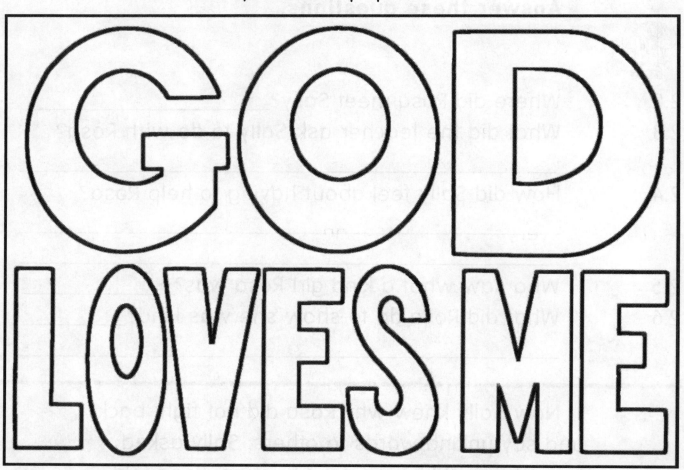

That night Rosa told Mama and Papa, "God has given me the Christian friend I prayed for." She was very happy for Sally and herself.

Sally still had much to learn about being a Christian. She had never read the Bible. She did not know how God wanted her to live. When she was unkind, she felt bad and wanted to act better. Rosa was a good friend and helped Sally to learn God's Word.

 Draw a circle around yes **or** no **after you read the sentences.**

2.8   We ought to love others because God loves us.

yes   no

2.9   We do not forgive others unless they forgive us.

yes   no

2.10   God sent His Son to die for everyone's sins.

yes   no

2.11   Everyone is a Christian.

yes   no

2.12   Only people who have trusted in Jesus as their Savior are Christians.

yes   no

2.13   All Christians are brothers and sisters.

yes   no

2.14   God loves me.

yes   no

2.15   You must be kind only to people who are kind to you.

                    yes   no

2.16   Christian friends can pray, love, and thank God
        together.

                    yes   no

Read the words ending with lt **and** sp. **Draw a line to the word that best completes each sentence.**

2.17   Stop when I say _____ .   grasp

2.18   My head has a big _____   felt
        on it.

2.19   She speaks with a _____ .   lisp

2.20   Please pass the _____   halt
        and pepper.

2.21   The sun _____ good on   wasp
        our backs.

2.22   Mother said, "Be careful or
        you will burn to a _____ ."   salt

2.23   I will pull you out if you
        will _____ my hand   welt
        real tight.

2.24   Wear a _____ with those
        pants.   crisp

2.25   It was no one's _____
        I got hurt.   fault

2.26   The _____ got into my
        shirt and stung me.   belt

BIBLE

3 0 9

LIFEPAC TEST

30 / 37

Name _____

Date _____

Score _____

BIBLE 309: LIFEPAC TEST

EACH ANSWER, 1 POINT

Complete First John 4:11 by writing the missing words.

1.   "Beloved, a. _____ b. _____ so
       c. _____ us, we d. _____ also
       e. _____ f. _____ one
       g. _____ ."

Draw a line under all true statements.

2.   The ways we are to treat others are:
      a.   serve them
      b.   love them with God's love
      c.   tell others about Jesus
      d.   share with them
      e.   make others do what we want
      f.   forgive them
      g.   be kind to the unkind
      h.   give others what they deserve

3.   Only Christians can
      a.   belong to the family of God
      b.   love God
      c.   belong to a big church
      d.   sing about Jesus
      e.   thank God for being saved
      f.   have eternal life
      g.   look like Christians

Write true **or** false.

4. _____ God takes care of you through others.
5. _____ Everyone is not in God's family.
6. _____ God is the heavenly Father of every Christian.
7. _____ Jesucristo is Jesus Christ in Spanish.
8. _____ Supplication is a long word for ask.
9. _____ Christians should never worry.
10. _____ Christians should pray about everything.
11. _____ Because God forgave you, you should forgive others.

Write a word from the Word Bank to complete each sentence.

Word Bank		
English	Christians	eternal
loves	thanksgiving	ought
Spanish	cousins	must

12. Brothers and sisters in God's family are _____ _____ .

13. You _____ to love others, because God loves you.

14. A Christian shows his love for God when he _____ others.

15. Life that lasts forever is _____ .

16. We should pray and make our requests known with _____ .

17. Rosa could not speak much a. _____ because she spoke b. _____ .

NOTES

GOD LOVES OTHERS THROUGH ME

The next day at school Sally wanted to have the book she had signed up for a long time ago. Someone else had taken it, and Sally knew it was her turn to have it. Sally became angry and told the teacher it was not fair. Sally told Rosa about the book. She was still angry.

Rosa told Sally that she knew it was Sally's turn for the book and that she was sorry someone else had taken it. She also told Sally to remember to please God. "Ask Jesus to help you not to feel angry. Ask Him to help you forgive the person who took the book." Rosa told Sally that God's Word says He loves you. Yes, Sally knew that. Rosa said, "Now that God lives in you, God can show His love for others through you."

Sally had to think about all the words that Rosa had said. She asked Rosa to help her learn verses to help her understand. Rosa wrote Ephesians 4:32 and First John 4:11 on cards for Sally.

Write the missing words.

2.27

(Ephesians 4:32)
"And be ye a. _____ one to another, tenderhearted, forgiving one another, even as b. _____ for Christ's sake hath forgiven c. _____ ."

2.28

(First John 4:11)
"Beloved, if a. _____ so loved us, we ought also to b. _____ one another."

Sally said she would let God love others through her. She forgave whoever took her book, and now she felt much better. It was funny, but she did not really want the book as much as she had thought she did.

Write what you think.

2.29   Why does God tell us to be kind to others?_____

_____

_____

Teacher check _____

                        Initial   Date

Study what you have read and done for this Self Test. This Self Test will check what you remember of this part and other parts you have read.

SELF TEST 2

Draw a circle around the word that best completes each sentence.

2.01   God loves others through _____ .
         people   houses   Christians

2.02   You _____ to love others because God loves you.
         can't   have   ought

2.03   You are the children of God by faith in
         _____ .
         your teacher   your papa   Jesus

2.04   You show others God's love by _____ words.

        big   kind   hard

2.05   A Christian should serve others because _____ says to.

        people   Mama   God

2.06   A Christian shows his love for God when he _____ others.

        loves   fights   hugs

Write First John 4:11.

2.07   "a. _____ if b. _____ so c. _____ us, we ought also to d. _____ one e. _____."

Draw lines to match these words and phrases. Then write the letter on each line.

2.08 _____ God loves   a. feeling kind toward others

2.09 _____ to work for others   b lasts forever

2.010 _____ tenderhearted   c. to have a duty

2.011 _____ eternal   d. me

2.012 _____ Jesucristo   e. serve

2.013 _____ Mexico   f. a country south of the United States

2.014 _____ ought   g. Jesus Christ

Complete these activities.

2.015   Write six ways you are to treat others.

a. _____

b. _____

c. _____

d. _____

e. _____

f. _____

2.016   Write why you are to be kind, forgiving, and tenderhearted toward others._____

_____

20	
	25

EACH ANSWER, 1 POINT

Teacher Check _____

Initial   Date

My Score

III. WHO WILL CARE FOR ME?

If Christians are to serve others, who will serve and care for them? Read on and you will find out.

VOCABULARY

supplication   (sup' lu kā' shun)   To ask for something.

Big flames came out of the windows of the pretty house. People were running down the street. Rosa could see her friend Sally crying and holding her dog in her arms. Rosa dropped her school books and ran to Sally.

"Oh Sally," said Rosa, "Thank God you are all right!"

Rosa put her arm around Sally and she stopped crying. They stood together for a long time watching the firefighters work. Finally, everyone was tired and needed to go home to rest. Sally looked at what was left of her home. She could not go home.

Rosa took Sally and her dog home with her. Sally's mother had been in the hospital for weeks and her father was still at work. He had left early that morning to visit her mother in the hospital. Sally was just leaving for school when she saw flames in the kitchen. She picked up her dog and ran outside crying for help. The neighbors called the firefighters. Rosa had just come by and found Sally holding her dog.

Sally stayed with Rosa for many days while her father tried to find another place for the family to live.

 Write the numbers showing what happened first, second, and so forth.

3.1 _____ Sally was just leaving for school when she saw flames in the kitchen.

3.2 _____ Sally went home with Rosa.

3.3 _____ Sally picked up her dog and ran outside crying for help.

3.4 _____ Rosa came and found Sally holding her dog.

Rosa and her mama and papa helped Sally to know that God did love her. They told her that God was her heavenly Father and that He would take care of her. They asked Sally to learn Philippians 4:6 and 7. "Be careful for nothing; but in everything by prayer and **supplication** [ask] with thanksgiving let your requests [things asked for] be made known unto God. And the peace of God, which passeth all understanding, shall keep your hearts and minds through Christ Jesus."

Mama told Sally that, "Be careful for nothing," means not to worry about anything. God knows everything. He will take care of you.

Write the answers to these questions on the lines.

3.5   What should a Christian worry about?_____

3.6   What should a Christian talk to God about?

_____

3.7   How can a Christian talk to God?_____

3.8   What does supplication mean?_____

_____

3.9   What do you give with your requests?_____

_____

3.10   Who do you make your requests known to?

_____

Write the missing words.

3.11   "Be careful for _____ ;

3.12   but in _____

3.13   by _____ and

3.14   supplication with _____

3.15   let your _____ be made
        known unto God." (Philippians 4:6)

Sally had many requests to make known to
God. She tried not to worry. She thought often
about God being her heavenly Father. She
wrote Philippians 4:6 and 7 on a card.

> "Be careful for nothing; but in every
> thing by prayer and supplication with
> thanksgiving let your requests be made
> known unto God.
>   And the peace of God, which passeth
> all understanding, shall keep your hearts
> and minds through Christ Jesus."
>   Philippians 4:6,7

Sally asked God to help her mother get well soon. She asked God to help her father find another house for them. She thanked God for her good Christian friends who were praying with her. Sally was learning to trust God more all the time. She was glad God was her Father.

 **Learn this verse.**

3.16   Learn Philippians 4:6 and 7. Say it perfectly to a friend.

Teacher check _____

Initial   Date

GOD WILL CARE FOR ME

Sally went to the hospital to visit her mother. Mother was feeling much better, but she was very worried and unhappy about the fire and being away from her family. She could see that Sally looked very good, even happy. She asked Sally what made her so happy.

Sally told her about having trusted Jesus as her Savior. She told her about being a child of God. She told her how God loves and cares for His children. She told her mother that God loved her, too.

Mother did not know what to think of all that Sally had said. She asked Sally, "How does God take care of you?"

Sally said, "God takes care of me in many ways. Rosa's mama said to remember these three:

1. God loves and cares for me through others.
2. God gives me peace of mind and joy even in bad times.
3. God will give me rewards in heaven."

Mother was still not sure about what Sally was telling her.

Sally brought a Bible to the hospital on her next visit. She showed her mother some verses to help her understand how God cares for us.

Fill in the blanks with the correct vowels.

3.17   Three ways God cares for me are
             a. thr____gh ____th____rs,
             b. thr____gh j____y ____nd p____ce of m____nd, and
             c. thr____gh r____w____rds ____n h____v____n.

Complete this activity. Sally's mother asked her why she was so happy.

3.18   Write four things Sally told her mother.
             a. _____
             b. _____
             c. _____
             d. _____

Complete this activity.

3.19   Do you remember the rule i before e except after c? Write the missing vowels.

             a. rec____ve   e. br____f
             b. bel____ve   f. ch____f
             c. rel____f   g. tr____d
             d. th____f   h. v____w

Write the words from Activity 3.19 on the lines to make these sentences correct.

3.20   I _____ that Jesus is the Son of God.

3.21   Look at the pretty _____ of the lake.

3.22   A _____ took all my money.

3.23   Did you _____ a phone call this morning?

3.24   Who is _____ of the tribe?

3.25   He _____ to do the job alone.

3.26   I hope John will come and give me some _____ .

3.27   This meeting should be very _____ .

Sometimes the /j/ sound in a word is spelled with a j as in jump.
Sometimes the /j/ sound is spelled with dge as in fudge.

Write the correct words from the list on the blanks. Circle the letters that spell the j sound.

lodge   budge   fudge
budget   smudged   dodge

3.28   The candy I like best is _____ .

3.29   I spilled the ink on my paper and now it is

_____.

3.30   When Father goes hunting in the woods, he stays at

a hunting _____.

3.31   No matter how hard I push, this door won't

_____.

3.32   When the boys throw the ball hard, I always

_____ it.

3.33   Buying that new dress really hurt Jane's

_____.

Sally's mother had many questions. Everyday she read the Bible Sally had brought to her to try to find the answers. She read how God loved her so much that He sent His only Son, Jesus, to die for her sins (John 3:16). She remembered that Sally had said God loved her and that He takes care of you when you belong to Him. Sally's mother wanted to belong to a God who loved her so much. She trusted in Jesus as her Savior. She told Sally's father about Jesus and he asked God to make him His child, too, through faith in Jesus. Now Sally's whole family belonged to Jesus. Sally was so happy. She knew God would take care of them.

Write down three ways God cares for you.

3.34   through _____

3.35   through j_____ and p_____ of
            m_____

3.36   through r_____ in h_____

Complete this crossword puzzle.

3.37   Write the answers to the questions in the puzzle.

Across

1. What is the name for Jesus Christ in Spanish?
2. What should a Christian pray about?
3. Who is the Saviour and Lord of every Christian?
4. What did Rosa call her father?
5. What do you do when you are happy?
6. What word means letting others use what is
    yours?
7. What can Jesus Christ do for others through
    Christians?
8. What is another name for Lord?
    Example: Lord Jesus or _____ Jesus
9. How do Christians talk to God?

Down

1. What does God give besides peace of mind?
6. What does everyone do that Jesus never did?
8. When people are unkind to you, what should you be to them?
9. What is the opposite of rich?
10. What should Christians give to God when they pray?
11. What is a long word that means "to ask"?
12. Who does God love through you?
13. Who is every Christian's heavenly Father?

Soon Sally's mother was well enough to go home. Sally's father had found a house for the family. Many friends gave them dishes, clothes, chairs, tables, beds, and many other things. This home was a very different home for Sally's family. It was not a beautiful home, but it was a very special home. It was full of love, God's love. So many people had been kind in sharing what they had.

Sally's mother remembered the three ways God took care of people—through others, by giving peace of mind and joy even in bad times, and by giving rewards in heaven. She could see how God had taken care of them through others and had given them all peace and joy even in the hard times.

Draw a line to show how God took care of Sally's family.

3.38	gifts from friends	joy and peace of mind
3.39	in reading God's Word	
3.40	in trusting in Jesus as Savior	rewards in heaven
3.41	in friends who pray for them	through others
3.42	in knowing God cares for them	
3.43	in having eternal life	

Rosa was very happy. She had many friends at school, now. The boys and girls wanted her to teach them Spanish. She brought many things to school to help the boys and girls learn about Mexico. She taught them how to make big paper flowers. The first Spanish word she taught them was Jesucristo. He was her friend and God was her heavenly Father. Rosa knew that God would always take care of her and now Sally knew it, too.

Study what you have read and done for this last Self Test. This Self Test will check what your remember in your studies of all parts in this LIFEPAC. The last Self Test will tell you what parts of the LIFEPAC you need to study again.

SELF TEST 3

Match these words and phrases.

3.01	requests	Christians
3.02	supplication	lasts forever
3.03	eternal	to ask for something
3.04	careful for nothing	not to worry
3.05	God's family	things that are asked for

Write the missing words.

3.06   "Be a. _____ for nothing; but in

b. _____ by c. _____ and

supplication with d._____ let

e. _____ requests be made

f. _____ unto g. _____."

Philippians h. _____

Write three ways God takes care of you.

3.07   _____

3.08   _____

3.09   _____

Write true **or** false.

3.010 _____ All people are God's creation.

3.011 _____ All people are God's family.

3.012 _____ Christians do not have to forgive others.

3.013 _____ God can love others through you.

3.014 _____ God cares about me only when I'm good.

3.015 _____ God gives joy and peace of mind.

3.016 _____ God cares for you through others.

3.017 _____ If Christians do not worry about some things, they will never get things done.

3.018 _____ A Christian should pray about everything.

3.019 _____ Because God loves everyone, we do not have to.

Draw a circle around the Bible verse where each of these statements is found.

3.020   If God so loved us, we ought also to love one another.

Philippians 4:6 and 7

First John 4:11

Ephesians 4:32

3.021   Be ye kind.
                Philippians 4:6 and 7
                First John 4:11
                Ephesians 4:32

3.022   Forgive one another.
                Philippians 4:6 and 7
                First John 4:11
                Ephesians 4:32

3.023   Be careful for nothing (do not worry).
                Philippians 4:6 and 7
                First John 4:11
                Ephesians 4:32

3.024   Be tenderhearted.
                Philippians 4:6 and 7
                First John 4:11
                Ephesians 4:32

3.025   Let your requests be made known unto God.
                Philippians 4:6 and 7
                First John 4:11
                Ephesians 4:32

How has God helped you?

3.026   Write about a time when God has taken care of your family._____

_____

_____

<table>
<tr><td>26</td></tr>
<tr><td>33</td></tr>
</table>

EACH ANSWER, 1 POINT

Teacher Check _____

Initial   Date

My Score

Review
REVIEW
Review

Before taking the LIFEPAC Test, you should do these self checks.

1.   Did you do good work on your last Self Test?

2.   Did you study again those parts of the LIFEPAC you did not remember?

     Check one: ☐   Yes (good)

                       ☐   No (ask your teacher)

3.   Do you know all the new words in "Words to Study"?

     Check one: ☐   Yes (good)

                       ☐   No (ask your teacher)